OVERKILL AND MEGALOVE

Overkill

CLEVELAND AND NEW YORK

NORMAN CORWIN

and

Megalove

THE WORLD PUBLISHING COMPANY

818.52
C832o

PUBLISHED BY THE WORLD PUBLISHING COMPANY
2231 WEST 110TH STREET, CLEVELAND 2, OHIO

PUBLISHED SIMULTANEOUSLY IN CANADA BY
NELSON, FOSTER & SCOTT LTD.

LIBRARY OF CONGRESS CATALOG CARD NUMBER: 63-8774

FIRST EDITION

Contents

OVERKILL AND MEGALOVE

Atom

NOW HEAR THIS:

All is atoms. Nit or man, whatever stirs with being is an arrangement of the microminimal.

Most atoms, however, just follow directions. Take hydrogen. Proud element. Building block of matter. Without it the oceans would no longer lust for the moon, would rend in two, gassify in a sheet of shock, one moment amplitudes of salted oxide, the next free and angry oxygen, with (from our narrow point of view) awkward consequences.

There are of course local zones within the atom, wards policed by subparticles. Any child knows this. And each is enthralled by the next, all bound by a tacit umbilicus of energy, and oh Jesus how they relate and balance and perform.

So you would think, wouldn't you, that inasmuch as the atom and its sublets are as basic as the first afflatus of creation when it sparked in God's head, you would think

11

that God would be zealous not to have them fringed upon by ignoranti.

For whatever we ultimately come to know, we shall never make so much as a successful clam or oyster, let alone a tree. All we can do is irritate and eat an oyster, never originate one.

Then who presumes to geld the neutron? Our Father who art in heaven? Why no, no, boobs and savants, intermingled, sometimes one and the same; and General Electric; and the People's Commissar in Charge of Fouling Posterity.

The atom obeys, fisses, fuses, enters into hot unions. And all would be well if it were not so resentful in the aggregate, and poisonous when provoked.

Power ships, yes. Light cities, yes yes. Suffer a sea-water change, unbrine bays, pipe same to faucet and field, yes yes yes. Coddle icecaps so Greenland may have its own Rapallo, go ahead if that pleases the Eskimos and Danes. Tag a cell, follow that spore, graph a goiter, nip a neoplasm, by all means. But kill and overkill is something else again and everything else on top.

And what do you think you are doing, learned and degreed professionals? You are nastier than the drunkard who pisseth in the street and viler than the hangman who enjoys his work. Ye are physicists of no value, miserable conformists are ye all, if you but polish the knob of the door to the chamber where strontium is armed.

And you of the camorra who tell us overkill need not be omnikill, and there will still be Smiling Jacks when it is safe to come up from the shelter, and thighs still hot to cover a woman, and seed still intromissible, seed unspotted

with puzzled chromosomes that contract blindly for un-
dulant malice down the generations,
O Tellers of such comfort, if there were only a conduit among
the natural hind-guts of the planet, of wide enough bore
to carry your gross message to the disposal area.

The Flaming Circle

A fire department which normally handles about 150 fires daily could not be expected to cope with over a million fires breaking out within a half hour [from a 20-megaton bomb striking Columbus Circle in New York City].
—TOM STONIER, *Nuclear Disaster*

Silence has virtues, but mainly for the weary ear.

It is entirely becoming to the grave alone, where all has been resigned and there is no proportion.

Its charms are wasted in the wasteland:

The blunt blatt of an auto horn, vulgar and mean on 42nd Street, would, if caromed among craggy bergs in the fastness of a Greenland night, seem blown by Gabriel or Roland.

Silence has its place and seasons, even its resorts, but one of them is not the city at midday.

Hence it is peculiar when the swarming isle is still, and nothing stirs save tainted air above the cooling grid.

No use dialing "0" in the emergency: the handset is molten and the party does not answer.

The megafire must consume itself: the fireman cannot put out the fire in his firehouse.

14

The peace needs keeping, but the squad car cannot see to it: the policeman is himself arrested in his tracks.

Beware updating of a Greek god's gifts:
Prometheus had good intentions, but his brand was a miscible blessing, like the apple that made the first two refugees.
Fire is a slave in a kettle, but a killer in the sky; it warms the baby's bottle, but cremates the nursery.

Only calipers that measure mountains can span the tongue-lick of a city crusher.
That last day of Pompeii was but the snore of an old giant who tosses in his sleep now and then.
Vulcan never presumed to be in all places at once—but his heirs pitch eruptions as a barfly in a pub throws darts.
The warhead homes to the inner circle of the living target; it does not ask of a bistro which way to the barracks: hence anticipations of fused glass from broken bottles, and scalded milk where the kitchen was, and the incinerated clientele.
The policy of a shock wave is to forbear dispute and hasten to its effect.
Once the edgy nucleus is butted from its dream of peace, nothing in the path is pitiable: the answering fire is not to be held in the hand, nor can a river quench it.

Flammable Rembrandts in the museum in the park:
Cleopatra's needle, perishable as the young camels in the children's zoo:
Rich men enterable into the kingdom of dust:
Hotel doormen braided like commercials:
Subway riders, done in by express intent:
Newspaper kiosks, their late editions later than was thought:

The spines of bridges broken, vertebrae trailing in polluted
   water:
Ships disemboweled against charcoal piers:
And, under girders and passive masonry startled into a state
   of shrapnel, or burned to various shades of coke and ash,
The megadead.

And in a control room thousands of miles away, a faint green
   quiver in a cathode tube, meaningful to the skilled:
And the word is passed up-channel: Bomb Delivered.
Then the break for tea, followed by demolition of the country
   as the first replies come down,
And negotiations continue for the end of man.

Cosmonautica

SEATTLE, April 6, 1962 (AP)—Russian cosmonaut Gherman Titov proclaimed Sunday his disbelief in God and said he saw "no God or angels" during his 17 orbits of the earth . . . "Some people say there is a God out there," the 27-year-old Soviet major [said], "but in my travels around the earth all day long I looked around and didn't see him. I saw no God or angels. . . . No God helped build our rocket. The rocket was made by our people."

When reached for comment, God said:

"Unfortunately I missed the orbiting of Cosmonaut Titov, which should not be held against me, since the Russians made no advance public announcement of his flight.

"At the time I was busy elsewhere creating a new sun roughly similar to your own, distant by a great many of what you call parsecs, from the scene.

"No slight was intended.

"The absence of angels is simply explained:

They were busy protecting the Chairman of the Party, the one who kisses returning Cosmonauts. There is a large vein in the region of his right temple which could pop under strain or upon hard drinking, and all the angels in the region who could be spared that day were helping him resist temptation, as assigned.

"May I add, it is perfectly true I had no hand in building the rocket. It was, as the major said in Seattle, made by his people.

"It was not the rocket I made, only the people."

Dr. Teller's Moon

WASHINGTON, March 27 (UPI)—Dr. Edward Teller told Congress today that the United States must, for its own security, gain control of the moon.

Dr. Teller, sometimes called "the father of the hydrogen bomb," coupled his warning with a plea for a program to establish a large and highly independent colony on the moon. He said the country that establishes a working base there could control near-by space, and would be able to "know what was going on everywhere on earth."

"We need the moon for our own safety," he told a House Science and Astronautics Committee. He also called for development of a nuclear reactor that could operate on the moon and might eventually provide enough power to extract water from its rocks and soil.

—*New York Times,* March 28, 1962

O Virgin Queen Selene
Mistress of the sun's shadow
Pearl of night's noon
Governess of love and lunacy
Eying us like God
Never turning your face away
Not quite trusting

19

These are orders: We shall set up on the shores of the Sea of
   Serenity a working base.
Specifications:
Barracks, hard by the pit of Anaxagoras;
Mortar emplacements bracing the Lake of the Sleepers
Antimissile missiles in a silo back of the Bay of Dews
Sidewinder battery on the dark side of Pythagoras
               In addition to which,
O orbed maiden with gunfire laden,
We shall colonize by crash program:
Housing project, coeducational, overlooking the Sea of Fer-
   tility
In Sinus Roris, a branch of the Chase National
Restricted preserves (test grounds) of the Atomic Energy
   Commission on the grand banks of the Ocean of Storms
Reader's Digest on the racks and vended Coca-Cola at every
   last PX
Plus nuclear reaction in the Lake of the Dead.

Pale Queen, so modest by day when the sky still rings with the
   brass of the sun
Yet even after the fiery old orb goes down behind the misting
   wests for still another round, leaving the purple dome to
   your uses,
Unfailingly you are discreet:
You cool the fevered desert
Warm by your faint breath the prostrate glacier
Stir fireflies in every wave and wavelet
Glow in the knowing night-eye of the cat.
Nevertheless, dear Madam, make no more nacre out of aery
   nothings and dull anythings,
For you must abdicate your silver throne.
Times change: try to adjust, Selene.

Now these are orders:

1. THIRST. Slake by roasting rock.
2. NEAR-BY SPACE. Command it.
3. NOMENCLATURE. Given names to stand: Tycho, Copernicus, Kepler, Ptolemy, and the like.
4. EXCEPTION to be made in the case of Crater Plato.
5. SUBSTITUTE FOR PLATO. Modesty forbids designation of substitutee in this communiqué, but designee shall be
    a) Naturalized American
    b) Nuclear Physicist
    c) Pre-eminent Cassandra.

This document is classified.

Legacy

The effects of the present bomb tests will
appear in the first generation of progeny,
and also in the second generation and
many future generations, not dying out,
even if the bomb tests were to be stopped
now, until after forty or fifty generations
have gone by.
—LINUS PAULING, *No More War!*

1.

What did your quarrel with the Trojans have to do with me,
    Agamemnon?
I am blind; there is a cancer behind my right eye, and I will
    not live to see my eighth birthday.
Did you have to throw that poisoned dust into everybody's
    air?
Couldn't you have settled your business with Priam, couldn't
    all that scandal over Helen have been negotiated?
You had warriors all around you: couldn't they fight like men
    and have done with it, and not sickened children like me
    three thousand years later?
It is bad enough that I will never see the sunlight you wasted
    on yourselves,
But my mother, who had hoped so long for a child, is going to
    grieve all her days because I, who was so promising, died of
    genetic defects you bequeathed to me,
There in your smug Greece so long ago!

2.

We have you to thank, gentlemen of Rome and Carthage,
for our monstrousness,
We of the incurable ward in the institution for defectives.
We know you did not begin it, that it began when Cyrus
dropped a token bomb on the Medes—or was it Nebu-
chadnezzar, earlier, on the Elamites?
Anyway it was to save Persian or Babylonian lives; we know
that; something about how many men it would have cost
otherwise to attack.
Then there was that naval battle, some seven hundred years
before Christ wasn't it, when Corinth used nuclear war-
heads on a limited basis against Corcyra.
But it was you, Rome and Carthage, that did the big-scale
testing, and you kept threatening each other; and after
Cannae there was no stopping and the bombs got bigger
and bigger.
And why, Hannibal, even in desperation, did you drop a
cobalt bomb? Was Carthage that important?
It hurts, senators of Rome and Carthage. Leukemia and idiocy
are not easy to live with or die from; and it rasps to know
that it all happened so far back, so very long ago.
Why, most of us don't even know what on earth you were
fighting about all that time.
Was it oil?

View From the Ark

NEW YORK—A Johns Hopkins University geneticist told the first national conference of scientists on survival of a little-publicized threat of nuclear war— the catastrophic upsetting of a combatant nation's delicately balanced biological environment. . . . In the absence of animal fallout shelters, lethal doses of radiation would erase all wild and domestic animals and destroy the nation's meat and dairy produce supply.

An even greater disaster would be the destruction of birds, because without birds insects would multiply "catastrophically." Insects, he said, together with bacteria are the only species "fitted for survival in the nuclear age." This is so because both are enormously radiation-resistant. Six hundred roentgens can kill a human but 100,000 "may not discomfort an insect in the least."

In the event of nuclear war "the cockroach will take over the habitations of humans and compete only with other insects or bacteria."
—*Los Angeles Times,* June 17, 1962

Noah, Noah, build an ark
Deep beneath the public park.
Gather bird and gather beast
But do not gather spores of yeast

24

(They don't need to burrow quite
As deeply as the adult white).

Noah, Noah, keep an eye
On the nation's food supply;
Beef you must insure, and milk,
But honey's safe and so is silk
Because, you see, the worm and bee
Are roentgen-radiation free.

Noah, you must leave behind
All that cannot be assigned
To be eaten by your kind:
Ornamental types like mink
Are out; do not even think
Of animals that spit or stink.

Noah, if you crave for liquor
Ark walls must be ever thicker:
Naught that ferments, grape or rice,
Will be left us—only lice.
Take on corn and store up cane
Else they'll not be brewed again.

Gather cottonseed for cloth
(Sheep will die but not the moth).
Dogs will die but not the flea
Tubers die but not TB
Trees will die but not the blight
Day will end but not the night.

Noah, make quite sure of fowl
Lest the cockroach form a cowl
On the crown of all the earth.

The crow is needed for rebirth.
All the Superbomb could will us
Would be virulent bacillus.

Noah, when you send the dove
To the blasted world above
Sheathe the bird in scales of lead
Till the Geiger counter's read;
If it comes back from the ride
Pray for God's insecticide.

Megalove

Love is lord of all the world by right.
　　　　　　　　　　—SPENSER

Not even basalt is tougher than the soft bedrock of life.

As device alone, what equals love?

The clock of cosmos, running on spiraled galactic main-
　springs? The pendulum that sweeps consolidated space?
　The force that pushes it?

The laser beam out of the excited ruby, lighting up the fillings
　in the molars of Mars?

　　　　　　(Thank you, keep your death rays.)

The rocket's orange glare, the thrust upward?

　　　　　　(Ice can shove harder.)

Computing machine?

　　　　　　(The brain cell is faster, stores more, and
　　　　　　feels pity.)

The articulation of the kneecap? Ball and socket in the chaste
　embrace of function?

　　　　　　(In the end, the joint stiffens.)

27

Billions of us hive on the rind of the globe; each knows his years are few, and nature hard.

He knows his span is a thin wedge between voids that cross in a running X at the point called Now

He knows the elongation of Then, and how it curves back along the arc of time.

He knows it is cold on the other side of the sky

And colder still, though not measurable by the usual instruments, only six feet down.

He knows that hellfire burns fiercer in the human breast than in the earth's hot core.

He knows he is born without his consent and dies against his will;

Yet lo, he loves, knowing—bitterest of all—that those he loves will sink to the grave before him, or—smallest of comforts—after him.

Each of us was ordained by an act of love;

And if here a parcel is less than tender, and there an unwanted birth,

These are but seaweed in the oceans of our breed

For Megalove is flood tide, thousands of millions of clasping embraces in a single night, in every single night,

Sea mounts and continents of locking limbs in a deep and shoreless Pacific.

Now if you please, beach the metaphor and dry it in the market place.

Say rather love is a staple in steady demand, mainly soft goods (though tougher than basalt, as already noted) and heavy with assets;

Persistently it issues common stock, each share coming to full term in the third quarter.

28

The desire of man for woman and she for him is in good
volume
Sons and daughters are bonds untradable
The love of brothers is ampler than car lots of grain,
long tons of copper
And in spite of what you hear, more units of fellowship
are moved each day than oil drums or iron ingots.

Megalove: the love of millions: and not only we.
Don't say it is just instinct when the whale gives suck to its calf
And the colt frisks at the flank of the mare
And the bear rears in fury when its cub is periled
Let none say love is traceless in the trout's milky sperm cloud,
a nebula richer than Pleiades,
Or when the fish tilapia carries his young in his mouth, as
careful not to swallow a son as a Mormon not to swallow
bourbon.

In the forging of lock and key for doors that open on earth's
green mantle,
Is not some heart in the work?
The invisible pageant of pollen, the fallout that spreads life?
Deny it only if you talk with seeds.

Look out over the city from the high escarpment of your brow,
and what do you see?
A mesa of stone, pincushion of steel, a grill of avenues.
The census at last count swore so and so many millions live
therein, gave the number of each gender, and the per-
centage of TV sets.
Well and good, but still unmustered are the figures on moist
lips and searching hands,
The declivities of bosoms, lusher than Kashmir's vale,

29

The caressing of waists incurved like the bouts of sensual
   cellos,
The games in the playgrounds of the senses:
Rooms lighting up in the mansions of the body;
And sighs, soft voices, let's not forget soft voices.

And the imagery in each head, the coinage of the heart
Whether love be to Her a wind on the water, a meteor shower,
   a beating wing, a hectic hour, a hornet sting
To Him the mane of a lion, a tiger's pride, high as Orion and
   twice the world wide . . .

All this, all this, and the babe in the crib,
And the awakening daughter, amazed to know she is in-
   timately related to the moon,
And the old man weary of the wearing down, only his affec-
   tions lying beyond the reach of sneaking sclerosis.

Love bulks like the Himalayas; the equator cannot girdle it,
It is fair in the darks of Africa and fecund at the poles,
It is a blanket resource of the planet, ambient and natural as
   air
                              and yet
                              and yet
                     oftener than often
The raw materials of love and amity are cornered and destroyed by half a dozen wanton wills: a Caesar or two; a
   restless general or two; a hero of the people by his own
   account; a moneyed puppetmaster
And five or six statesmen, that's all it takes, make it seven
   at the outside:
Old men mostly, past fighting, their kidneys in decline,
Their speech a diplomatic parsley dipped in the blood of the
   young:

> "Accept, sirs, renewed assurances of high con-
> sideration.
>
> "His Excellency wishes to acknowledge
> receipt of your communication of the 10th
> December, and to assure you that his Govern-
> ment has no intention of interfering with the
> integrity of your sovereign people."

The lingo is polite as varnish,
Sincere as the wax-faced undertaker saying, "We are sorry
    about your loss."
And after the notes are exchanged, and high respects trans-
    mitted like wires on Mother's Day,
WAR COMES!
And where megalove was a flood of sparkling waters,
Megadeath is the tide run out, and stinking mud, and carrion,
    and rotting hulks,
And the bones of lovers, and the curled fists of quite dead
    infants.

O God! Scatter thou the people that delight in war!
Do not the pikes of the regimented years club us down fast
    enough?
And cruel chance, and want, and force majeur of fire and
    flood?
Do not the tiring and stumbling heart, the rampant cell, slay
    hosts enough
Without gratuitous war?

Do as the Psalmist begged you, God of love, you have the
    means:
Scatter the guts of those that delight in war
For they, the few, the parsley eaters, asses in gorilla skins,

Caesars riding tigers they dare not get off,
They are annihilators: love is no safer than nations.

If you do not scatter them
We shall have to.
And it will be bloody as usual.

Non Sequitur Trumanensis

> INDEPENDENCE, MO., March 3 (AP)—Harry S. Truman said today President Kennedy "is on the right track" on his decision to resume atmospheric testing. "It was the proper thing to do. We should never have stopped it. Where would we be today if Thomas Edison had been forced to stop his experiments with the electric light bulb?"
> —*Washington Star,* March 4, 1962

Why, Harry, we'd be where your father was, reading his
    Bible by gaslight
Or where young Lincoln was, reading law books by the glow
    of a fire in a fireplace
Or where the audience in the Globe was, watching royalty
    carve each other up by lampwick,
Or where Homer was, writing in Greek sunshine.

Fallout

> Radiation from test fallout . . . might be
> slightly beneficial.
>> —DR. EDWARD TELLER,
>> *The Legacy of Hiroshima*

Praise fallout, O my soul, and forget not all its benefits.
Especially downwind.

First roentgens fall out, then the hair.
> What is so bad about that? After all epilation is local:
> happens only in the same state where the bomb goes off;
> and, if you live six months, the hair grows back.
Further downstream there are other, greater, more enduring
benefits:
> The busy strontiums (89 and 90)
> Common carbon souped up to scintillate (isotope 14)
> Iodine (131) with grander talents than to paint a bruise
> against infection
> And cesium (137), fickle metal (explodes in water
> ordinarily but is silent in air when disguised as fall-
> out); invisible and circumspect; enters the reproduc-
> tive organs quietly
> And stays.

What child prefers dull, healthy bone
When strontium can light it up?
Ah, the secret emanation in the marrow: waking and sleep-
ing and at play it is there, busy busy busy, tirelessly busy
They say that cancer comes of it and leukemia but this may
well be propaganda: don't think it and you won't get it.
Coo, baby, where you are glowing in the dark, kicking your
feet in the cradle,
For on the X-ray plate you will show up lit like a holy city,
like a star cluster, twinkling blue peanut brittle,
Like a Christmas tree out in stupid space where no man
passes.

Exceptions

Brothers, we are brothers all
Except for one or two:
The nigger and the indian
and then of course the jew.
For every one the Open Door
O, welcome all alike!
Except the chink and several more
Including spig and kike.
Equality for all, for all,
Except for six or eight
We love our neighbors every one
Except for those we hate.

Ready? Ready!

> The world is not ready for nuclear dis-
> armament, or any other kind of dis-
> armament.
>
> —DR. EDWARD TELLER

In the year 2076 at last the world was ready for disarmament,

And the word went out

And from Asia and the Americas, the delegates, all four of
them, came to meet in the stump of a gutted city among
degraded Alps.

And the delegates from the Americas said they spoke for the
entire population spread out across the hemisphere—perhaps three or four hundred people all told; and that
although most of them were sick from disorders of the
blood and bone marrow, those who were competent had
expressed the wish to ratify the disarmament treaty.

The Asian delegates replied that in behalf of the sovereign
people inhabiting the vast land mass between the Baltic
and Pacific, amounting to eighty-seven persons including
six children, they were equally ready to accept the treaty
with only minor qualifications, these to be negotiated before final ratification, but that to all intents and purposes
their attitude could be construed as an agreement in prin-
ciple.

And then the delegates from the Americas asked whether anywhere in the Asias there could be spared any whole milk for the children on their side,

And the Asians replied that though their own needs were sore and pressing, they would be willing to exchange some quarts of whole milk for pints of whole blood, needed for transfusions for the six leukemic children of their own.

The exchange was agreed upon (subject to ratification on both sides of course), but before the conference adjourned two delegates collapsed and died from malnutrition, a third succumbed to sudden virulent infection to which he lacked resistance, and the fourth from internal hemorrhages induced by derangement of the clotting platelets in the blood;

And it was some time before their bodies were discovered, along with the minutes of the meeting. By then the remaining home populations were so weak that the disarmament treaty came into use automatically.

It is still in force today as I, the last human being before my species becomes extinct, write these few words for whatever intelligent beings may chance to visit this planet from dis

Midsummer Night's Unplumbed Dream

It was in the last McCarthiad

And my Japanese gardner, who understands no English but smiles happily at everything I say,

Handed me a letter on a silver tray as I was sitting out on the lawn retching.

I opened it to find a message from a Watussi who had just come down to the left bank of the Niger on the annual trek for salt.

His style was British colonial, thanks to agents of the London Missionary Society, and he wrote in part as follows:

"The theatah is for Entertainment. People don't want to go to a theatah and feel bedly. The gravamen of my advice is that the *Diary of Ann Frank,* as adapted by the Hacketts, will never go in Mgubi."

I rose unsteadily from my bed of thorns and staggered to the pool.

The filter pot was sucking air in hideous screeching gulps because the water level was low (city water with some

Sr 90 in solution, naturally, from a series at Christmas
Island)

And lo, there in the middle of the pool was the excised
bladder of a playwright, being used by a critic's child as
a floating toy.

As there is nothing too revolting to enlist my interest,

I bent over to inspect it; instantly I was challenged by a
professional palmist who had somehow sneaked up behind
me.

"I charge only one hundred dollars for a reading," he said.

"What if I don't like the reading and refuse to give you the
money?" I asked.

"Then you don't get your palm back."

He gave no sign of leaving, so I told him I was Pisces with
Sagittarius descent, and that got rid of him.

The venue changed at this point to a fashionable suburb on
the estuary of the Styx.

The tall spare boatman who rowed me over did not seem to
think I would ever make it back, what with the radiation
and all.

From afar I heard a wail like a busy Friday night at the
wailing wall, and I looked and saw a group of my countrymen aghast before an illuminated cliff of Dow Jones
averages.

Suddenly it came over me that there were other things in
life: I resolved that I would never play house with any
girl whose bra stays in place all the time, for that can be
monotonous.

On the nether shore were two ladies who seemed to recognize
me. One said, "I would bow from the waist but it snaps
the whalebone in my bustle." And the other said, "Believe me, the happy ending is more commercial."

Then a Pope appeared out of nowhere, Sam Pope, with a

head like Caesar Augustus and a beard like Lincoln's, and as he kissed the tassles of a tallus he said, "The common people must love God, they made so many of Him."

Then within my dream I dreamed that I had been spitted on a coaxial cable, and was slowly roasting over a brisk bonfire of napalm. I felt this was uncivilized procedure and said so in no uncertain terms to the foreign office.

"Why are you doing this to me?" I demanded (through my spokesman, Lincoln White).

After many a summer came back a crisp note reading,
"You see a cloud in back of every silver lining. You point with undue alarm, whereas alarm is not due until it is meet to press the panic button, not before."

I stood in disbelief. The Styx was gone, together with the tank farms of Esso gas and Modess ads explaining Why.

In their stead stood the collected works of my Aunt Mildred, which dissolved presently into a pageant of all the poetry and drama from Ionescu to Becket, in Cinemascope ratio,

And around the waist of the Times Building flowed an electrified legend reading, "Any war today, anywhere in this tenderized, tinderized 360-degree ammunition dump

Has to be the sum of the squares of both sides."

Symptomology

The disease of which the hydrogen bomb
is a symptom is the continuous and apparently irresistible march of technology
which makes all kinds of weapons pro-
gressively more simple, more versatile,
and more lethal.
    —FREEMAN J. DYSON, *The Bulletin
      of the Atomic Scientist,*
    September, 1961

One and one are two
And two and two are four.
You could go on forever thus
But it would be a bore.

TNT is fast
Fission even faster
But fusion is more versatile
And vaster, vaster.

When the world is ill
It only needs a knock:
Technology for discipline
And hydrogen for shock.

42

If you have a dream
Of orderly pursuit
It matters not that when in heat
The atom is a brute.

It is a fact of life
That thanks to sickly art
It's easier as time goes on
To blow the world apart.

Joke Section

1.

In September, 1961, the Soviet Union broke a voluntary moratorium on the testing of nuclear weapons that had been jointly kept by itself and the United States for three years. On October 31, 1961, the Russians tested a "terror weapon" estimated to be at least 50 megatons in strength. Later Premier Khrushchev at a meeting of the 22nd Congress of the Communist Party boasted that because of a "mistake," the bomb had actually been much stronger than anticipated. "But we are not going to punish our scientists for that," he said, at which the delegates to the Congress laughed heartily.

A funny thing happened on the way to the crematorium.

There was this radiated corpse, see, and as the hearse rounded the corner on two wheels, it fell out of the casket and rolled around on the floor.

We all laughed.

Well, two of us put on lead gloves and lifted it back into the coffin, being careful not to expose our middle to transpirations from the hot stiff

Because as you know carbon 14 can get you in the gonads

And when we had restored order, so to speak, we sat around

44

kidding about the Politburo and the NKVD, and swapping
stories about Nikita,
And since the ride was a long one, and the wheels got stuck
from time to time in mushy asphalt (from the radiance
of the last atmospheric test)
We had plenty of time for yuks.
There was this Academician who won the Order of Lenin
for his studies in Biblical history
And he told us that Ruth the Moabitess the wife of Boaz
was actually a revolutionary who held up a bank in Moab
to furnish funds for a Yemenite Actors' Studio.
We laughed again.
Then a Geneticist of the People, winner of a Medal of Merit,
said that although there are such things as dirty stories,
there is no such thing as a clean bomb,
Which also struck us as funny.
At about which time we came to a train crossing and found
a dozen freight cars scattered about where there had been
a collision, also passenger coaches on fire, with citizen
travelers roasting inside, and both locomotives lay on their
sides with burst boilers,
And a Comrade Deputy, who had come along with us just
for the ride, studied the scene for a moment and then
remarked,
"What a hell of a way to run a railroad."
It was so spontaneous and witty that we all writhed with
laughter until the corpse, a little slow to get the point,
joined us;
And a real good time was had by all.

2.

On fallout [Dr. Edward Teller] said there was more possibility of genetic damage in people wearing a pair of trousers than the change forced by nuclear testing at the present. Teller said Linus Pauling, a foe of testing because he considers the dangers of fallout very real, does not wear kilts to protect himself from the danger of trousers.

—UPI Dispatch, June 11, 1962

Grab humor by the short hairs, Doctor.

Genetic damage being seated in the scrotum, make a smallish joke, so small as to be infinitesticle.

Killing With Kindness

> It is conceivable that radiological warfare could be used in a humane manner.
> —DR. EDWARD TELLER and
> DR. ALBERT LATTER,
> *Our Nuclear Future*

> *humane*, 2. Having the feeling and inclinations creditable to man; having, showing, or evidencing a disposition to treat other human beings or animals with kindness or compassion; benevolent. Humanizing, exalting, refining.
> —*Webster's New International Dictionary*, second ed.

The times are not so far gone as to begrudge little acts of
    watchful courtesy.
See how the earth's old seamed face freshens with each kind
    service shown:
Between hale men a warm handclasp is a secondary means
    of grace,
The primary being a humane bomb, small and almost clean,
Discreet and prim like the one that diffused remembrances
    over Hiroshima.

> *Those who were watching the plane had their
> eye grounds burned. Most are third degree, so
> cure is impossible.**

---

* From *Hiroshima Diary*, by Michihiko Hachiya, M.D.

47

It was in its way exalting, at least upwind of the blast, from a tram window in a suburb: creamy and apocalyptic so long as the image did not sear the eyeball.

> *That beautiful cloud! It was neither red nor yellow. Its beauty defies description.*

Alas, not a joy forever—but then much beauty is like that: the pearly nimbus fades, the sunset leaches into night, the rose gives up its tincture. So must the passionate cloud exhale its substance amidst bewildered airs.

> *"Obasan, did you find your son's bones?" "Well, I found some bones still steaming, but I began to wonder, and so returned the next day and looked again. This time, I knew they were his because I recognized his belt buckle."*

It was such a little fellow
(The vintage A-bomb, that is, not the missing flesh around the steaming bones)
A rascal, really, alongside the Doomsday apparatus that today can deal ten thousand times more roughly with any city-state.
The modest flare that lit the Honshu morning, was by any fair compare, compassionate.

> *I ran into four middle-school students who were badly burned. They sat in a small circle beside the road, and I stopped to ask one where his home was. He replied that this was his home and asked that if I should encounter his mother and sister would I tell them not to waste their time looking for him because they were all going to die. Next morning I took*

some things I thought might add to their
comfort, and searched until I found them.
They were dead, huddled in the same small
circle.

Boys being boys, they used to run a mile to see a fire, but on that August morning they ran to get away from several, and were very tired at the end.

Fire is punishment. Somehow they were culpable, these children, somewhere they had crossed a code and broken it: a full demerit to them for having chosen to be born in the same bristling epoch as Premier Tojo and General Groves; another mark against their names for picking, out of all the places in the world to live by, the banks of the Ota.

Wiser children would have had their mothers come to term in San Diego.

I was disturbed most by the sight of burnt
toys in the ruins.

Again, demerits: instead of playing with their dolls and blocks (a frivolous waste of national hours) could they not have swayed the secret program of the obscure ministry down in the crypts of the Imperial Government?

The wages of childhood delinquency are napalm, shock waves, and gamma radiation.

O David, warring David, son of Jesse, put down your interregnum harp and answer whether, in that hushed hour when you sang, "I lie even among the children of men that are set on fire," there had been an extra quiver in the strings; whether they were brushed perhaps by the wingtip of some mournful angel who foresaw cyclonic inclinations toward a distant isle.

One old woman I saw on rounds annoyed me
because she kept asking us to end her life.

She had not been injured, was in no pain, and out of respect for her age, everyone tried to make her comfortable, but her only response was to ask everyone who came near, to end her misery. Her family had been killed, and she was alone in the world.

There! Who needs more hearty proof that humaneness is conceivable in fulminating atoms? Grandmother was untouched, uninjured, in no pain. The bomb had scolded others, but it showed compassion for her; only her own querulousness was an inconvenience to the maimed and dying. (Old people are like that; blow up their city, and they whine.)

There can be manners to the scorching neutron. Though it blister tile routinely, it will spare a painting of Whistler's Mother out of thoughtful computations and refinements.

Flowers follow.

They had no faces! Their eyes, noses and mouths had been burnt away and it looked like their ears had melted off. One soldier, whose features had been destroyed and was left with his white teeth sticking out, asked me for some water, but I didn't have any.

A few adjustments to be made toward humanizing radiological war:

Along with ruptured islands, fragmented cities, bridges blown off their buckled piers,

Melted statuary, activated ashes of the public parks and markets,

Something new: refinement:

With each blast, prosthetics:

A shower of sutures and skin grafts, settling out of the mush-
room of indiscriminate debris:
A gentle rain of jawbones restored to jaws; ears pinned back
on; mouths good as new, built up around the teeth;
Noses from a nose bank,
Also water, preferably uncontaminated, should a faceless
man be thirsty from the fever of the bright occasion.
It would take some doing to compound these features in the
formulation of the humane bomb,
But Science is a prodigy:
The child may yet (conceivably) surpass its Maker,
Though it might be well for us to purge our sins before the
day it happens.

> *There were so many burned the odor was like
> drying squid. I have never seen so pathetic
> a spectacle. . . . The swimming pool is filled
> with dead people . . . Even the playground
> was packed with the dead and dying. What a
> pitiful sight it was to see them lying there in
> the hot sun.*

Humaneness is filterable:
The quality of mercy may conceivably be strained from
fission products. Thus, where man's pity has been jaded
from disuse, the bomb will quicken it. If the spectacle of
people rendered into squid wakens pathos in the breast,
has not some good been done?
When in the pool and playground the forbidden game is life,
and a neighborhood of neighbors lies depleted from the
rigors of the contest,
May one not proffer thanks for this special kindness: that
pity, which is famous as sworn servant unto love,
Is roused. If pity now, then love tomorrow; and,
Since love by reputation conquers all,

The bomb, by softening the sensibilities, broadcasts humanity
   as a farmer spreads manure,
Each molecule of dung committed to the cheer and comfort
   of the seed.

I

I never saw a bomb
Nor understood MC
Yet know I how a mushroom looks
And what a blast can be.

I never spoke with Nik
Nor felt an atom's breath
Yet certain am I of the end
As if its name were Death.

II

"BLOOD" screamed the sirens and the Strike-First pro-
   ponents
"BLOOD" screamed the skull-faced, lean War Ministers.
                    BOOM kill the pygmies
                    BOOM kill the Arabs
                    BOOM kill the white men
                    WHO WHO WHO
WHO killed Cock Robin?
WHO killed the peace plan?
WHO killed the last disarmament proposal?

Barrel-house Niki with feet unstable
Sagged and reeled and pounded on the table,
Pounded on the table,
Beat an empty issue with the handle of a broom
Hard as he was able,
Boom boom BOOM
With umbrella clauses and a threat of doom
Boomlay, boomlay, boomlay, BOOM.

III

The bomb comes
on little cat feet.
It obliterates
harbor and city
and raises a cloud
which then moves on.

IV

At the Hijiyama High School in Hiroshima, 51 girls were outdoors on the
school grounds . . . They were all se-
verely burned, and the mortality within
a week was 100%. The mortality among
shielded school children was 14.2%, in
contrast to unshielded children whose
mortality was 83.7%.
　　　　　—TOM STONIER, *Nuclear Disaster*

With rue my heart is laden
For girls of the event
For many a slant-eyed maiden
Unshielded by cement.

By acts too old for weeping
The young ones are in bed:
The children now are sleeping
Percentages of dead.

V

All I could see from where I stood
Was three deep craters and some mud
I turned and looked another way
And saw a city dripping blood.

VI

A thing of beauty is a joy for as long as will be permitted by the international situation.

VII

Some say the world will end in fire
Some say in ice.
From items on the AP wire
I hold with those that figure fire.

VIII

This is the way the world ends
This is the way the world ends
This is the way the world ends
Not with a whimper but a bang.

IX

Oh, East is East, and West is West, and the twain had better meet.

X

A Doomsday weapons system might be imaginatively (and entirely hypothetically) described as follows: Assume that for, say, $10 billion we could build a device whose only function is to destroy all human life . . . The computer would then be programmed so that if, say, five nuclear bombs exploded over the United States, the device would be triggered and the earth destroyed. Barring such things as coding errors (an important technical consideration) the above machine would seem to be the "ideal" Type I Deterrent.

—HERMAN KAHN, *On Thermonuclear War*

In Xanadu did Herman Kahn
A fearful atom bomb decree
Whence Alpha radiation ran
Through fallouts measureless to man
Down to a poisoned sea
So twice five miles of fertile ground
With crater walls were girdled round
And where were gardens bright with sinuous rills
And blossomed many an incense-bearing tree,
Are now strewn corpses out of Overkills
And fragments of Doomsday machinery.

A savage place; as disenchanted
As e'er beneath a Teller's moon was haunted
By woman wailing for her blasted lover!
For from this chasm, with ceaseless fission seething,
As if this earth its last thick gasps were breathing,

A mighty mushroom momently was forced,
Amid whose swift unintermitted burst
Huge fragments vaulted like rebounding hail,
Or contaminated grain beneath the thresher's flail:
And 'mid the smoking rocks at once and ever
It flung up momently the bloody river,
Five miles meandering with a mazy motion
Through lifeless plains the polluted river ran,
Then reached a reading measureless to man,
Because no man was left on land or ocean:
And mid this tumult Herman heard from far
Ancestral voices prophesying war!

With warnings loud and long,
I would test that bomb in air,
That awful bomb! those beds of salt!
And all shall die who see it there,
And all should cry, Beware! Beware!
The flashing sky, the floating beir!
Weave a circle round me thrice
And close your eyes with holy dread,
For I on hypotheses hath fed,
And drunk the brew of Poltergeists.

Subways of the World, Unite!

The hypothetical Columbus Circle hit would create a hole in which a 20-story building could stand without showing above ground. One could expect the blast wave to literally clean out the entire underground-connected portion of the subway system. A blast wave travelling in a tunnel loses its energy much more slowly than travelling through open air. This stems from the fact that the blast waves are continuously reflected back from the walls of the tunnel.

—TOM STONIER, *Nuclear Disaster*

Moscow has the Louvre of subways.

Had Bernini been Ukranian and Michelangelo an Uzbek under a Five Year Plan

Piazza Novotny, fruity and fountainous, might be underground at Kropotkinskaya Station

And God (which is to say V. Lenin) would be muralized in the act of touching a divine finger to Stalin on the vaulted ceilings of a cultural express stop.

The subways of New York, on the other hand, are of bare proletarian tile, with gumgobs on the platforms, and candy-vending machines (also peanuts) clasping pillars that hold up streets.

Numbered stations envy the lilt of Kaluzhskaya Zastav and the mournful music of Botanichesky Sad;

There is no blare of trumpets in the cry of Flushing and
Flatbush:

But who shall cavil if the trains are on time and the freight
delivered?

Under London and Paris too, inelegant burrows: though
Boston's be the dean of undergrounds, never a Cabot
would lodge in it, not even for the spell of an alert, nay,
not even to descend from rains of debris or radiation.
Certain things a gentleman must not do.

Among subways is a rooty understanding, a brotherhood of
moles: what happens in the overworld is crustal and
superior, and none of their assignment, save in war.

Closest to Charon and his ferry slip they lie; farthest our
God from thee:

They dam the rushing hours, sluice a few into the flush of
Rush Hour, work their level peristalsis in the bowels of
the earth.

Now we are told a bomb would purge you,

Ream you clean of tracks and frescoes, vestibules and escala-
tors, chiclet cubes and people.

Object. Resist. Blast waves are harsh enough in open air,
and crudely literal toward connected systems of the upper
ways.

To amplify what is already more than ample is redundant,
like the overkilling of passenger pigeons:

Yet here are reflections on reflections from tunnel walls,
promised like craters and carcinoma

And the names of stations guaranteed to be garbled in a
ghastly anagram, their mosaic tiles indistinguishable from
prosaic cinder.

So rise, you subways, rise like a sidewalk lift, like a dumb
waiter that has found its voice

Splay your veins and turn them skyward like a strip mine

Strike! No turnstile turn, no token taken, no electric shoe
scuff power from the vital rail
Until all bombs are drowned in trenches deep as Mariana
And only the fires of decent and natural hell, bearing the seal
of Dante's approval, burn in the nether levels.

Subways of the world, unite!
You have nothing to lose but your trains.

Landscape Before Crashing

> At the scene of the crash he called for
> his "Mommy and Daddy" and said "My
> mother is waiting for me" [at the airport]
> . . . He told of looking out of the plane
> window at snow falling on the city, just
> before the crash. "It looked like a picture
> out of a fairy book," he said. "It was a
> beautiful sight."
> —*New York Times* report on Steven
> Baltz, young boy from Wilmette, Illi-
> nois, who was the only survivor of a
> jet plane collision over Brooklyn on
> December 16, 1960. He died soon
> afterward.

Considering the repertoire of war, and how it is played in
   some theater somewhere almost continuously
The entire flight pattern is unsafe for children.
Ours being the only passenger conveyance in the system
   (the rest of the planets transport mainly rock, marsh gas,
   and—in the case of Mars—possibly algae), we have no
   other choice than to carry our kids with us if the race is
   to persist
But still it is a shame to bring them aboard at all if it is just
   to give them a glimpse through a plastic window of the
   fascinating landscape, and then smash them into the
   ground.

   From the air most cities, even grubby ones, look like
      pictures out of a fairy book, and in winter when snow
      that makes snowmen and snowballs falls on them and

covers their warts and birthmarks, they are indeed a beautiful sight.

So is the rest of the world a beautiful sight, Steven, in all seasons.

It is here in this world that you can walk, jump, run, swim, skate, ride a bicycle, shoot aggies, draw, paint, put together model airplanes and hi-fi sets, feed pets, and read the funnies

Here are silly putty and hula hoops and pogo sticks and baseball averages and Bozo

It is here in this world that Mommy is waiting at the airport while you ride on a powerful jet that owns the sky like Superman

And on the ground in that fairy-book picture there are movies to be seen and Radio City, and a keeno elevator that whooshes a hundred stories to the top of the Empire State Building, with a terrific view from the top and telescopes

And Daddy knows how to get to the Statue of Liberty, and maybe you will stay in a tall hotel, where all you have to do is dial "3" on the room telephone, and a man comes and gets your laundry.

There are also many beautiful sights, Steven, as you grow up and your voice changes and a beard casts its shadow before. There are trees that bud green in the spring like yourself; and the girl you're sweet on; and her lips when you nibble at the first kiss for either of you;

And even for grownups there are beautiful sights, more beautiful sights than you can shake a stick at, and beautiful sounds, too; and it would take too long to tell you about even half of them, so you'll have to accept our word for it.

But the trick is to reach the airport. Lots of kids have never done it. Not through any fault of their own, Steven, any more than it was your fault when two blind planes piloted by grownups crashed in the air that luckless snowy day in December.

Lots of kids were luckless enough to be born in London and Coventry and Warsaw and Rotterdam and Hamburg and Dresden and Hiroshima in the early forties, and not one of them asked to go on the ride,

Yet there they were, passengers without knowing why or where to, playing what games they could play and learning what their elders felt they should be taught—alphabets and numbers and manners and how to get down to the shelter and all like that,

And they just about had time to peek out of the window at the big and mysterious world around them when there was a big bang and a crash of metal and beams and plaster, and they were permanently separated from their Mommies and Daddies.

Clean it up, gentlemen.

When you are through bandying casualty tables as though calculating the tuna catch

And plapping on typewriter platens the census of projected dead

With extrapolations hot from the computers, as to ratios between megatons and overkilling;

After you have arrived at the going rate on endemic slaughter

And demonstrated how we can survive Survival

Then let us have a version for the kiddies. To explain to them the dragon-infested hazards of just living and breathing and minding their own games

Years before they could possibly offend a foreign ministry.

Spring Song

Now the sun is a friendly brazier under a thawing sky
And the grass shines and the bird sings because it is in him
    to sing
And the night players, the crickets and frogs and cicadas,
    rest in their tenements, drugged by the drone of locusts,
    not to be roused until the evening cues,
And the leaf elaborates gold beams into green blades
And the worm is in a heaven of humus
And dragonflies patrol on private urgencies, stitching dazzled
    orbits
And the fern stirs and the frond dips in an idle brook of air,
And nothing that is dead knows it is dead.

O love, lie by me and let us look through the humors of our
    eyes into the measureless countries that we call our own
And with our lips and tongue tips set seal against the prying
    of words, for sweeter conjugations.
Your breasts and their soft sisters shall outwear the granite of

the Appalachias, and my hands are happy serpents seeking
    contours
Pillow my head like a cloud in the hollow of your bosom
    where the eager drums of the heart sound clear
The belly of a sail is fair, but yours is fairer, and glows with
    the knowledge of a million Eves: moreover it is dimpled:
Your thighs are what temple columns in Attica hope to be
    when granted life; they meet at a Corinthian capital above
    the Mount of Venus.

Love, this being spring, let us make a child
And God damn the bomb.

Now About That Next War, Son

> When a child wants to know about war,
> what does a parent say that is honest,
> clear and meaningful? How can we avoid
> either deception on the one hand, or a
> distressing confession of our immaturity
> on the other? . . . The next war could
> easily exterminate mankind. Children to-
> day feel that the adult world has not
> solved the problem of living together—
> only of dying together.
> —SIDNEY J. HARRIS, *Chicago
> Daily News*

Take him aside and tell him Yes, we are in it together:

The rich with their automatic comforts, and the family
bunking seven in a room:

The trained, who understand poems and cybernetics, and
the boys in leather jackets who browse through comic
books at the corner newsstand:

Old people tired of wars and winters, and children who do
not yet know they are made of matter:

The famous face in four colors, nationalized on the cover
of the magazine; and the crowd face, the background face,
gray, nameless, out of focus:

We are in it together.

Tell him the secrets of the earth have been peeled, one by
one, until the core is bare:

The recipes are private, in guarded codes, but the stink of

death is public, as always when orders come down for
the big kill.
Tell him no covenant is so openly arrived at as that between
the murderable masses and their murderers.
Tell him there have been improvements since the good old
days of Nagasaki; that the atom can be more sullen than
has yet been shown:
Attack it with another thrust of algebraic symbols and the
cutting edge of an equation, and there may well be the
Grand Reaction:
The first news of it will arrive in our region as a shuddering
in the sky: a glow, far off, brightening, heat beating out-
ward in concentric waves, the atmosphere a band of fire,
the seas themselves, the wet seas, tinder:
The hills which looked on Christ will heave and crackle, and
quarries vaporize as meekly as the dust of Pharaohs:
The earth, the tamed and tonsured earth with all its gardens
and substances, it places, breeds, and patterns, its letters
and it airs, will plummet out of grace, will fail its orbit:
And soon enough will be a blistered ash, its moon trailing
ungoverned like a dog after his master's corpse.

Tell him we are all in the zone of danger: in it together:
Seat Belt Fastened:
The crackpot prophet stands at last within reasonable pros-
pect when he picks a date and says, "On This Day the
World Will End. Selah. Repent Ye Sinners, and Prepare."
Tell him what has become of the victors and their victories
And how those who spoiled for war were spoiled for peace:
Tell him how epochs hang on the tailored charms of diplo-
mats:
Tell him how we should have learned by now that every
multiple of one comes to but One in the arithmetic of
nations:

That unless we work at it together, at a single earth,

There will be others out of the just-born and the not-yet con-
tracted for, who will die for our invisible daily mistakes.

Tell him there will be others, but with this difference: Next
time, the fighting heart shall be unemployed: shall be re-
placed by a coil of wire: the secret weapons of the spirit
rooted out by a pound or two of restless elements:

Valor no more is the truss of armies:

The regimental banners, the Order of the Day, the skill of
killing drilled into the recruit, the encampments, the
massive embarkations—they are but extras in the package
deal of war, the silos full of arson and the deadly plagues.

Now the control board and its buttons, the air-conditioned
laboratory, dustless and remote, by the waters of the wired
lake: these are the armed forces.

But tell him also that alarm is easier than pride to point with:

We are in it together, and that, when held up to a certain
light, is good as much as ill:

For Oneness is our destination, has long been: is by far the
best of places to arrive at:

That the signs along the way, at Galilee and Philadelphia and
Gettysburg, said ALL CREATED EQUAL

STRAIGHT AHEAD
KEEP GOING
STICK TOGETHER
ALL IS ONE

The chemicking that could destroy us can also do as bidden
by us: outmaneuver genii: be servile to the meek: reform
our wayward systems peacefully.

Tell him the choice rests in the care of what fragile peace
we have: including his trusteeship, if he but live to his
majority:

One, or nothing: wealth, or laying waste:
Men, or Jew and Gentile: men, or the color of men:
These are the choices, and we make them daily.

Tell him he must learn to answer for himself.

Tree-Speech

A fig tree come forth in its nudity gleam-
ing over the dark winter-earth is a sight
to behold. Ah, if it could but answer!
or if we had tree-speech!
—D. H. LAWRENCE, *Sea and Sardinia*

How to endure on the earth.
Well, when the tilt of the globe awakens us each spring
We extol living. We put out blossoms and scatter riches and
    are no poorer for it.
Out of the cloud comes our chemistry.
In the lash of the storm we grip harder.

Whereas you, all your days you finger coins and buttons,
    locks and switches.
Your paths are macadamized, your walls piped and wired,
    you are in with the machine.
Your skies are sooty. Sewers wait for the rains of heaven.

Here, beyond the squall of your freeways
Unhurried roots pry in clay and sunder rock
Constellations of fruits are planned in secret chambers
Leaf and needle negotiate with the near star for growth and
    green
Time is easy.

76

What news there is, is of such making as the slow explosion
   of the seed: as wings released from chrysalis: as programs
   in the almanac of bud and cycle: rhythms of the zodiac:
   the sentimental senescences of autumn.

We're sorry for you, but wish you well.
It should only be that tribes of trees descend with your
   children
To a day when the shade of the oak spreads wider than the
   shadow of war.

Now you say something.

Not Choose Not

Not, I'll not, carrion comfort, Despair . . .
. . . ór, most weary, cry *I can no more.*
I can;
Can something, hope, wish day come, not
choose not to be.
                    —GERARD MANLEY HOPKINS,
                         Carrion Comfort

Only the cowardly imagination gives us over to the crucible.

To believe peace impossible is the surest way to make it so.

Now that the common denominator of extinction is at least
    a nation, and birds of ill omen drum impatient wings where
    they brood in the aviary of gloomy science,

It is worse than carrion comfort to embrace Despair in
    public: maggots are invited to the feast.

Beware those ancient airs on how man's instinct is (and will
    forever be) manacled to war:

A libel on the race; for never did an army englut the tedious
    manual of arms except by brazen mandate and maneuvered
    inspiration.

Indifference is a costly luxury: its soft cushion but a head-
    man's block.

There is the mortification of the letting go: sullen confusion,
    and the washing of hands.

The game can be resigned at any time: a dozen sleeping pills from hand to mouth, and the board is clear of every menace.

God, like negotiations, can be cut off too.

Think small, and you will come to mousehood:

It is easy for the state of peace to have an ant's horizon: you need only be a member in good standing of the anthill, running this way and that, feeding the fat queen of suspicion:

For despondency yaps the cry of attack as shrilly as the general who lusts to strike first with the biggest overkiller.

Death has a good name in the provinces of fear.

Nothing can be done by doing nothing:

Better a dream, a hope, a pale petition, a wish-day-come,

Better to take a stand and take your lumps for it

Than build a shelter against the facts of physics, stocking it with biscuits and a cylinder of Cyklon-B, in case it's kinder to the children to go that way.

The due rank of peace is proudest above all earthly dignities.

Believe it, and ensue it so.

Could Be

Foreword

One has a right to be dismayed by the ugly and deadly thermonuclear arts, but it is a waste of feeling to be depressed. What might conceivably help is to think of peace as potentially strong instead of weak and piping, as capable of being articulate, equipped, and rugged, rather than stammering, naked, poor, and mangled.

"War," observed Thomas Hardy in The Dynasts, *"makes rattling good history, but Peace is poor reading." That being the case traditionally, we should perhaps think about reversing the tables. The thought occurred to William James in a powerful essay entitled* The Moral Equivalent of War, *written around the turn of the century, but there were few if any seconding voices. In a medium that did not exist in James's day, I tried a variation on the theme. In 1949, at the behest of the United Nations (to whose informational arm I was attached through the high-sounding portfolio of Chief of Special Projects), I wrote and produced a not-so-fantastical*

fantasy entitled Could Be. *Only political obstacles, not technical, make the canvas at all utopian.*

But somehow political obstacles are never in the way of global undertakings whose end is the sanctioned murder of millions; or of gigantic crash programs involving national prestige, which are astronomic both in nature and expense. To reach the moon or Venus is obviously more dramatic, hence apparently more desirable, than to reach understanding with one's own world. Space, like war, makes rattling good reading.

Don't ask me *how good the reading is, of the hitherto unpublished adventure which closes this volume. I am disentitled to answer that question because I wrote it; still, it is only fair to report that it apparently made good listening when it was twice performed over an American network, and subsequently heard in Britain, Canada, and Australia. The most significant of the responses to these broadcasts (also the most treasured) came from one of the few men in history qualified to comment on the negotiability and practicability of* Could Be's *premise: Fleet Admiral Chester W. Nimitz, who commanded the greatest naval operation in the annals of war. Admiral Nimitz wrote me after listening to the broadcast, "I wish not only every American but all foreigners could hear it."*

Perhaps on the strength of the admiral's approbation, the publishers and I are justified in proffering it as one kind of spiritual antidote to the rampant poisons of fission-fusionism —if not on those grounds, then as a working demonstration, however imperfect, of the posse-pursuit of peace to which we all are exhorted late in the preceding pages.

I choose not to think Could Be *is a pale petition, but instead a Hopkins "wish-day-come"; and who knows, if the wishing be earnest and deep and wide enough, it might happen.*

84

Could Be *is of course a break from the style of the fore-*
going pages, but no break from the burden they attempt. I
wrote the earlier matter as pieces, not especially as poems,
and will be neither flattered nor offended if the reader ushers
them in or out of this or that group of genera. In the same
spirit, I wrote Could Be *under no arbitrary heading such as*
Fantasy or Documentary, though it certainly combines ele-
ments of both.

In selecting geographical arenas for the action of the script,
I did not arrive at them by spitting in my hand and striking
the palm with two fingers. I asked the specialized agencies
of the United Nations, those that would stand to be recruited
in such an enterprise, exactly where they would go to work
and what they would do if actually given the chance and the
means to potentialize the world along the lines envisioned.
They answered, "Middle East, Amazonia, Yangtze Basin."
Nor did I guess at the technology involved: there is absolutely
nothing antic or visionary about the methods and physical
objectives depicted. For example, the basis for the aero-
generator wind towers was a set of plans drawn up by the
United States Department of the Interior, and introduced to
the UNSCCUR Conference (United Nations Conference on
the Conservation and Utilization of Resources) in 1949.
Where I was called on to exercise my own imagination was
in the dramatization of the big push, the form it took, the
elements that comprised it, the timing of the "invasion," the
deliberately calculated "sensationalizing" of the project, and
details of the communications roundups both before and after
zero hour.

Though the text was fourteen years old at the time of
writing these notes, nothing has had to be "updated" except
for the accommodation of television instead of an exclusively
audio (which is to say, radio) pickup. Today, through satel-
lites of which Telstar in 1962 was prototype, legible images

85

could hypothetically be transmitted from all remote points in the communications system of the Task Force enterprises. Also, an apparatus nonexistent at the time of the broadcast, the atom-powered ship, has for some years now been an actuality. I wish I could say that the rest is history. It is not. But with good will, dedication, and a little bit of luck, it could be.

Could Be

> Peace hath her victories no less renowned
> than war.
>
> —MILTON

VOICE: (*Out of darkness*) This comes to you, in a sense, with the compliments of the future. It is based on what could be, in the lifetime of most of us; based on what is now known and scientifically possible. It is a dream view, a storyboard, a synopsis of what could happen if the nations of the world got together and attacked common problems with the same vigor, determination, and resources with which, from time to time, they have attacked each other.

Suspend your disbelief for long enough to belong to a time that could conceivably arrive—a future whose distance from now need be only as long as we make it.

Come in, year X . . . come in . . . come in . . .

> *Fade in: the thronged rooftop of the Secretariat Building at United Nations Headquarters. Appointments not ordinary to its routine existence have been improvised for a*

87

OBSERVER 1: Greetings.

For those of you who are just joining this transmission, we are broadcasting from the roof of the Secretariat Building at the permanent headquarters of the United Nations overlooking the East River in New York City.

There is naturally great excitement here in anticipation of the long awaited zero hour, of the so-called Peace Blitz that the world has watched building for so many years. Though it is not quite ten in the evening along the eastern seaboard, it is fourteen minutes before dawn in that distant part of the world where the combined forces of Task Force One will strike at conditions that have kept that area, and regions like it, in darkness and depression for thousands of years.

I repeat, it is now about fourteen minutes before zero hour; and in the intervening time we will bring you pickups from countries where, just as here in the United States, people are awake and in holiday mood, awaiting the transmission that will carry word of the dawning, not only of a new day, but of a new era.

We take you now to Observer Number 2 on the terraced roof gardens above the Assembly Hall. He will describe, from a better vantage point than I, the scene before us.

OBSERVER 2: You are looking down on an amazing sight, a sight that was certainly not envisioned when this lot of real estate was opened to the UN back in 1951. The lights of this incomparable city are ablaze, and the skyline stands prouder than ever. As you can see there across the river, the Astoria side is lit up also. That big soft-drink advertising sign that dominated the Queens landscape when the

UN plant was built is still there, although it has since been surrounded by some equally big signs.

Directly below, on the base extending from First Avenue to the water's edge, people are thronging the Park area. I don't know whether you can make out the full extent of the crowd, against the glare from the light towers just across from us. On Roosevelt Drive cars are crawling both ways, bumper to bumper—seems as though every motorist in the city is out tonight to look at these floodlit buildings, these monoliths in which the main planning for the Blitz has been done.

Perhaps you can hear above the noise of the crowd music of the orchestra which all evening has been playing tunes of various countries. We have a camera down there, and if time permits—

OBSERVER 1: (*Interrupting*) Sorry, but time will not permit. Satellite signals are now being received from Down Under —and we take you to Wellington, New Zealand.

Sound of atmospherics momentarily; a few flickering images, then a steady picture.

WELLINGTON: Hello, UN, New York. I am speaking from the auditorium of Victoria College in Wellington, the capital city of New Zealand. Here it is 2:24 in the afternoon of a day which is even now racing toward its appointment on the Euphrates, halfway across the globe between you and us.

Wellington has broken out in bunting. This is ordinarily a placid city on holidays, but New Zealanders, like most other people who voted overwhelmingly for the Blitz, are visibly enthusiastic over the prospects to be opened up before this day is over.

The music you hear is from a chorus of Maoris—there

89

is a good shot of them now—the original inhabitants of New Zealand. They are chanting an ancient haka, as a greeting to all our viewers. Listen to a moment of it:

A rousing, rhythmic chant of infectious warmth and power, punctuated by shouts and the stamping of feet.

And there's our good luck wish from New Zealand to the Task Forces on the Euphrates, Amazon, and Yangtze. We take you now to Seattle, Washington, U.S.A.

Again, atmospherics and some fluttering of images on the switchover.

SEATTLE: This is Observer 3 speaking from the bridge of the recently launched S.S. *Madame Curie* at her berth in Elliott Bay, Seattle harbor. It is nearly seven in the evening here, and the floodlit ship is surrounded by small craft. In just about thirty seconds we will hear the first whistle of this first passenger liner in the world to be run by atomic energy.

As you may know, the maiden voyage of the *Curie* is timed to begin some nine minutes from now, as soon as sun is up on the Euphrates. The trip will take her eventually to all three of the Blitz areas: the Middle East, the Amazon, and China.

The crowd down on the pier, and the ship's crew around us, are listening for *Madame* to find her voice, to speak her first word through a blast of steam raised by heat from the atomic pile in the innards of the ship. The order to blow the whistle will be given by the captain to the executive officer, who will then push the button that controls the whistle. You will probably be able to—

CAPTAIN: (*Off*) Mister, blow one long blast.

90

A profound ocean-liner whistle, followed immediately by answering whistles and the tooting of a number of smaller craft, over which:

SEATTLE: The *Madame Curie* is now being cheered by other craft in the harbor, and a great din has been set up. We take you now to London, England.

A smooth switch. Parliament Square lit up like a night baseball game (or cricket match).

LONDON: This is London.

I am speaking to you from Parliament Square. Here in the shadow of Big Ben and the House of Parliament we are at the heart of the city. It is nearly three in the morning, and yet to judge from the crowds along Whitehall and on Westminster Bridge, one would think it was high noon. All the way up to Trafalgar Square a great crowd has gathered to listen to the wireless and watch the television report of the tremendous event due in less than nine minutes from now.

Across in Central Hall on the other side of the square there is in progress an exhibition of the United Kingdom's role in the World Task Forces, showing just how men and supplies from these islands are contributing.

Camera pans up to face of Big Ben.

Over our head, the minute hand of Big Ben is moving toward the hour. In about forty seconds, the old clock, imperturbable in war as in peace, having struck punctually through all the various moods and cycles of history, will acknowledge three A.M. as it has done tens of thousands of mornings before this one.

But if, wherever you may be, you should detect an extra resonance in Big Ben's ring this morning, it may be in

91

appreciation of the fact that before he strikes again, the world will have struck its own new hour—the hour in which international differences are for the first time subordinated to a massive popular peacetime effort benefiting all nations, big and small, rich and poor.

It is now twenty seconds before three o'clock, Greenwich Time.

Big Ben strikes the hour.

From London we take you to the city of Lourenco Marques in Mozambique, East Africa.

Mozambique does not come in. We see snow, grain, tweed, and various other patterns on the TV tube, and hear a general wash of static, but there is no picture.

Come in, Mozambique.

More of the same. Something has gone wrong.

Come in, Mozambique, East Africa.

Nothing. These things happen.

Calling Radio Mozambique, East Africa. Do you hear us, CR7BG?

If it does, there is no indication.

Ladies and gentlemen, owing to circumstances beyond our control, we are unable to contact Mozambique. We take you now to Warsaw.

A clean move. This is more like it.

WARSAW: This is Warsaw. It is just after four in the morning here. I am speaking from a dizzy position atop a steel girder on a building that is just two rivets away from completion. When finished, this will be the world's biggest combined solar radiation and heat pump plant, designed to help keep Warsaw comfortable in the winter by using the warmth of the ground and the sun.

Although this is a strange hour for construction to be going on, the workers on this project got up a petition last week to hold off the hammering of the *last* rivet until zero hour this morning, so that they could sentimentally tie in with the start of the invasion a few minutes from now. For the purposes of this program they asked that the *next-*to-last rivet be used as a sound of greeting to the men and women of the World Task Forces. The last rivet, they will drive home the instant the sun rises over the Euphrates, by which time this telecast will be there too.

The rivet is being heated now. In the meantime, as you can see perhaps, there is enough light in the wide-awake city below to make out something of it. There is a big crowd in Soski Place, waiting for a fireworks celebration to be touched off at zero hour. Off to the west is the Memorial to the Warsaw Ghetto, bathed in golden light.

It has taken many years to restore this most thoroughly devastated European city of World War II, so the people of this country have special understanding of the differences between invasions of war and peace.

(*Animatedly*) There goes the rivet! It's just been thrown by a heater to the riveter—I hope you were able to see the beautiful fiery arc it made in the darkness. And now in a mo—

> *The bone-rattling sound of riveting; closeup (Zoomar lens) of pneumatic drill hammering the rivet home.*

And that's all from Warsaw. This is Poland sending the program along to Paraguay in South America.

93

A little fuzz; not bad.

PARAGUAY: (*Over pleasant music of that country*) Good evening from the village of Ajos in Paraguay. I am an Indian from the Chaco, and I am invited by Paraguayan Radio to speak now. That music you hear is my friends, sitting around a fire out here in the open. It is a song of peace which they sing.

We know something of war here in the middle of this continent. Once there was a war in Paraguay which killed eighty per cent of our people—killed more than one million people in a country of one million and a quarter. But, who today in other countries remembers when that war was, or why it was fought? Nobody. It was a waste.

We like peace and plenty, and that is why we voted for the Blitz, like everybody else. This is a small village in a small country, but two men and one woman from here are tonight in the Euphrates Task Force from where we will hear a broadcast in very few minutes from now.

The song in the background ends.

We wish everybody good luck. Now you go to Paris, the capital city of France.

> *A confused sound of merrymaking, shouts, babble, comes in before the picture, but the delay is slight.*

PARIS: Bon jour, bon jour, bon jour. I am speaking to you from the top of the Arc de Triomphe, and you are looking down the Champs Elysées toward the Louvre. Oh, how I wish our camera crews could spend some time showing you how the rest of Paris looks this beautiful morning. If it was ever gay, it is gay this moment, this very hour. Earlier tonight we had a procession, a carnival, just like they have in Nice in southern France, and also in New Orleans in America. Great floats showing the work to be done under the plan of the Peace Blitz. You should have seen the float on atomic energy, with the lights shining up from it like heat waves, and the model wind towers also, and the hydro dams with—how you say—damsels on top of them. (*Laughs at his own small joke.*) But we must not delay to return you to UN Headquarters in New York.

> *Clean switch, except for a brief, rapid flop-over.*

OBSERVER 1: Thank you, stations. We have just received word that the executive secretary of the Economic and Social Council is about to make an announcement. We take you to Council Chamber 4:

> *The interior of Council Chamber 4. The Secretary is surrounded by officials and reporters, none of them identified. He rather broadly acknowledges the cue that his camera is on the air, with an unnecessary nod.*

SECRETARY: Good evening. Throughout the planning stages of this enterprise, we of the Economic and Social Council were perfectly aware, as are most of you, that there is by no means unanimity on the method chosen to establish a new era of progress. It was therefore recommended by the Council that on this broadcast the opponents of the operation be permitted, in the spirit of democratic fair play, to state their case. We have just located and are now able to bring you the President of the World Advancement Federation, whom we now pick up in Finland, where he is on a speaking tour.

Come in, Helsinki.

The face of the leading opponent. He is grave, dignified, and persuaded.

OPPONENT: Thank you for this gracious gesture in offering the opponents of the Blitz project a chance to be heard by your world-wide audience.

None of us in the Federation wishes to deny anybody the enthusiasm and hopefulness which have been aroused. But we are deeply concerned lest this enthusiasm be short-lived and, after the first exhilaration of this costly adventure, the world be let down. Let me briefly number our four main points:

1. It is frivolous to stage a mock war in this fashion, since there is no tangible "enemy" to attack, in the sense of a hostile army.

2. When you suddenly change ancient methods among backward peoples, and shatter their established patterns of living and thinking overnight, certain frustrations are bound to result.

3. The cost is fantastic. To mention only a few items: two billions to inoculate every person in the world against some disease or other—with or without his leave! Sixteen billions for dams, factories, irrigation! A billion dollars to build *privies* for every family in the world that hasn't got one! It's a staggering investment, without any guarantee of return!

4. The whole scheme smacks of sensationalism and dramatics. Since nothing faintly like it has ever been attempted, and you have no sure guide of experience, failure may result in a paralyzing discouragement of progress in the future. We believe you are disseminating false hopes, and that from your megalomania, little good can come. That is all. Thank you, and good morning.

FINNISH VOICE: We return you to United Nations Headquarters in New York.

No hitch. We are back in Council Chamber 4. The Secretary has a paper in his hand, on which he has made notes. He refers to them as he replies:

SECRETARY: Thank you for these interesting views. We should like to reply to them briefly, in the order in which they were presented:

1. The enemy is indeed tangible. Disease is an enemy. It has killed more people than armies. Undeveloped resources is an enemy. As many wars have been fought over needed resources as for any other reason in history.

2. The sudden shattering of established patterns of illness, hunger, and poverty is going to frustrate nobody except those who prefer, for whatever reason—and there are surprisingly many—to perpetuate conditions of illness, hunger, and poverty.

3. Yes, the cost is admittedly high. To clean up the world *is* expensive. It costs as much as a small fraction of what it cost to destroy most of the world in the last two wars. However, it's not a question of what it costs, but of what is best for us. A sanitation department is unproductive and never returns a penny, but it isn't very nice to live without one. Besides, economists have shown that the investment will ultimately pay itself back five hundred to one thousand per cent—some of it even before the work is finished.

4. Yes, the plan *is* sensational. It was *intended* to capture the imagination of the world, and it has done that. As in wartime, peoples have set their minds on a goal, and therefore they will accomplish things never attempted in

the past. Also, as in wartime, large things will be done quickly by large numbers of people in a large effort. We are disseminating seeds and knowledge, and from this, magnificent results can come.

May I just add that only to an extremely skeptical acorn does the prospect of a forest of mighty oaks seem megalomaniac.

Thank you very much.

> *The control returns to the rooftop of the Secretariat Building.*

OBSERVER 1: (*With suppressed emotion*) This is Observer 1 again on the roof of UN headquarters. It is exactly thirty seconds to zero hour, and the cheering crowd in the park areas below has quieted with the realization of the approaching moment. A hush is spreading over the entire area, and traffic has come to a stop; people have dropped their voices and stopped moving about in order to hear what is soon to come through the loud-speakers, and be projected on the mammoth screens set up at a dozen locations.

The signal—a pure oscillating note—will mean that the communications circuits to the site of the far-off event are open. Following the note—which is due in seven seconds from now, the control will automatically switch to the scene—five seconds. . .four. . .three. . .two. . .one. . .

> *The sound of a high, keen oscillator note; a very slight transmission hum; a cloudy image on the screen, which quickly clears.*

HILL 1: I am speaking from the summit of a high hill looking down on a land older than the Bible. The light of approaching day has just begun to suffuse the sky to the east. In about one minute's time the sun will edge over the rim of this bleak and desolate terrain.

Below us in a two-mile-wide pass through which courses the Euphrates is massed an Army—you can't see it yet in the darkness—the first in history to invade a country with instruments of life, not weapons of death—to construct, not destroy.

(*Looking through binoculars*) As the valley grows a little brighter, I can make out through these glasses the divisional banners—the various national flags—the UN flag—all streaming in the wind.

On this hill is the Co-ordinator of Task Force One, whose rank corresponds to that of Generalissimo. As soon as light breaks, trumpets will announce the Order of the Day which the Co-ordinator will give by short-wave radio to amplifying trucks along the valley. I imagine you will be able to hear echoes of his voice from the sound trucks ranged at various distances along the valley.

(*Excitedly*) There it is!—There is the first glint of the sun! The sun is rising! . . .

> *Distantly, very distantly, from the valley below, the sound of bugles . . . a variation, peaceward, of the traditional battle charge. When its last reverberations have faded:*

CO-ORDINATOR: (*His voice echoing in a series of retreating perspectives from the valley below*) Men and women: You go forth to restore the earth; to heal the sick; to liberate man from poverty, hunger, and fear of age; to instill in untried peoples the confidence to do superb things for themselves.

Do your job well, knowing that the hard-won dreams of the world rest with you.

A distant roar, as of thousands of engines starting up.

CONTROL: Now we can distinctly hear the sound of motors. The first rays of light are slanting down the valley now, and the Task Force, stretching as far as we can see, has begun to move forward. We transfer you now to Observer 3, standing on the floor of the valley.

> *Cut in on an enormous roar of engines; on the screen, clouds of dust through which only intermittently we are able to make out the individual tractors, bulldozers, and heavy equipment.*

OBSERVER 3: (*Shouting to top the noise*) Hello! Hello! I hope you can hear me! Can you hear me? I can't hear myself above the roar of these motors all around us here!

The whole force, the whole army is moving east, up rising ground . . . moving at a good clip for this kind of gear. Grinding by us now are whole squadrons of cats, bulldozers, half-tracks, tractors, trucks—there's no end of 'em. The drivers and crews are shouting and laughing and waving their hands, and there's an air of extreme excitement.

The tractors are already leaving the formation at the head of the column, and fanning out north and south, with the object of terracing the lower hills. They know exactly where they're going, because every bit of this ground has been studied and mapped by advance units. Now bulldozers are breaking away from the main column and heading for the river, where they'll slash into the low banks of the Euphrates to clean out mosquito-breeding bush. I've just had a signal to transfer you to Hill 2 on the western side of the valley. Take it away, Hill 2.

The waspish drone of small planes flying at low altitude, some of them taking off at an airdrome whose runways are just coming into the light.

HILL 2: I am standing on Hill 2 from which we can see to the north an airdrome where planes are taking off to join the procession. They are flying due east over the ground forces, and no doubt you see them as they flash past the summit of this hill headed for special targets. That one— the one that has just caught the light on its fuselage— bears the emblem "WHO"—meaning World Health Organization. It's on its way to spray malarial marshes. Just overhead now is a squadron of photographic planes making a record of the invasion for newsreels and archives; and there's one with the FAO legend—Food and Agriculture Organization—on its way to drop wheat seed over land around Kirkuk. I understand one of the first FAO rice planes is over a near-by objective and is ready to drop seed. We're going to contact it for you—

Come in, FAO Pilot 17.

What at first seems to be a fast blur resolves itself quickly into a landscape whizzing past, as seen from a camera mounted on the plane.

PILOT: (*A woman*) Roger. I'm flying this plane alone, with an automatic camera under the nose, and I'm descending to twenty feet as I approach Field 14. There's a hopper under my seat, holding a half ton of rice seed, and all I have to do is push a button to start it going, and the seed will run out and be scattered by propeller backwash.

There are two flagmen standing down there at both ends of the field to guide me, and they're waving at me now as I come in. I'm just about over the first flag now, and here we go—I've tripped the hopper, and rice is streaming out behind; and in the time it takes to tell this I'm practically at the far end of the field, and I'll have to climb now before turning.

She does climb; as the plane banks, the horizon tilts at a rakish angle, then straightens out again. There has been no interruption in the pilot's commentary.

At this rate I can plant a whole acre every ninety seconds, which is a lot faster than the old method—and besides, you don't get your feet wet. That's all from here—

Over to you, Control.

CONTROL: This is Control back at Hill 1. We have heard from the jet plane, the *Einstein,* now en route from Karachi, where it took off at dawn, Pakistan time. We will have a direct pickup from her as soon as she is over this area. It is from the *Einstein,* you know, that the new dam is to be inaugurated. I'm speaking of the hydroelectric dam at Deir-Ez-Zor, which was finished last September, and is waiting to turn its impounded waters into the desert for irrigation. The gates of the dam will open at the moment the *Einstein* passes over it. However, this is still some minutes away. First, to Observer 4 in the village of Qaryah Ghariyab—Over.

A group of villagers, most of them plainly or poorly clothed, clustering about an observer who carries his own microphone. Tables covered with food are in the background; also women carrying flowers.

QARYAH: I am speaking from the old village of Qaryah Ghariyab where I live. I am a citizen of this country being invaded. The whole population is already out along the

102

Tikrit road to welcome the Task Force supply division in which are so many of our own countrymen.

Camera pans to accommodate his description.

The streets here are practically deserted except for a few old people. Also the village Cassandra, who I am afraid is going to scold us.

An old woman in a black shawl comes up and delivers a scolding harangue in Arabic. Observer 4 takes it in stride, as part of the scene. C'est la paix.

This woman says she is sure that fighting has broken out ahead and is coming this way. She refuses to believe what her neighbors tell her—that what looks and sounds like gunfire in the distance is just dynamiting for construction of the new water-supply system through here.

The women of the village, as you can see over there, have prepared a fine honorary luncheon for the supply unit expected here by noon. I can smell the food from where I stand.

Well, hello and goodbye from Qaryah Ghariyab. Back to Control.

Control comes in instantly.

CONTROL: Thank you, Number 4. We've just picked up on the monitor a report that the fishing trawler *Ole Baake,* in the Gulf of Oman, twelve hundred miles southeast of here, is ready to come in. The *Ole Baake,* incidentally, is named for a UN mediation guard who was killed in the Palestine trouble back in 1948—Come in, Observer 5, in the Gulf of Oman.

Long shot, from an accompanying vessel, of a trawler idling through a glassy sea. After a moment, we come up on the craft itself. A camera is mounted in the bridge, from which our commentator speaks.

TRAWLER: This is Observer 5 on the bridge of the *Ole Baake* in the middle of the Gulf of Oman. We saw the *Einstein* pass overhead about an hour ago, headed north, and looking mighty pretty and cool up there. I don't mind telling you it's hot and humid enough down here to stew a turtle. But when it gets up around 120 degrees Fahrenheit this afternoon, we'll just stick our heads in the automatic freezing tunnel below. It's 50 degrees below zero down there, and the fish get frozen stiffer than a board as they pass through the tunnel on a conveyor belt on their way to storage bins. We also pipe some of that cold into our living and sleeping quarters, so it's not too bad.

Up here in the chart room is a radar device—

Camera goes to it.

which locates fish, just as in war radar was used to search out submarines. That "blip" you're hearing is a signal that a school of salmon is ahead of the ship at a distance of— oh, about—wait a minute, I'll ask—

MATE: (*Off*) Fifteen hundred meters.

TRAWLER: That's about five thousand feet ahead, to port. This echo-ranger and sounder is really very talented—can identify not only the position, but the kind of fish—whether it's shark, tunny, mackerel, or whale—they do have whales in this gulf, you know. It tells how deep they're running, and also the speed at which the fish and the ship are approaching each other. (*Muffled voice off*)—What you say?

104

MATE: (*More loudly*) We're chasing sardines, not salmon. No salmon here. India oil sardines.

TRAWLER: I'm corrected. What's coming through on the radar is a school of India oil sardines, not as I previously said, salmon. Anyway it's fish, and it's going to help feed people.

That what you want, Euphrates? Back to you up there!

Hill 1 again. The landscape is quite bright and clear now, though it is still early locally.

CONTROL: Thank you, *Baake*. We've got a report from the *Einstein* that she is over Haditha to the south of here and will be over the formation in a matter of minutes. Meanwhile, let's have a word from an observer in the middle of that formation. Over to 6.

Heavy equipment as far as the eye can see, all moving: men, dust, heat, noise, great good spirit.

SEED: It's very exciting to sit on a half-track carrying hybrid corn seed, and watch the world move into action along with you. There are hundreds of vehicles around us in a tremendous cloud of dust, and I was able to identify the flags of fifty-three countries before I lost count. There's a communications unit—construction unit—educational squad—a mobile hospital has just bounced past us. Followed by a library on wheels. Right behind us is a division of carpenters, and in front of us a team of veterinarians on its way to set up animal-control centers, wherever needed. The nearest thing to a suggestion of *war* in this Blitz, far as I can see, is the extermination squad, which is moving ahead in a grim, determined way. I'm going to pass Control along to one of these workers. Over to you, 7.

105

Another part of the forest of equipment.

EXTERMINATOR: All we're out to exterminate is rats, bugs, lice, vermin, and locusts. We're the ground force of a crew that includes spraying by air, and our planes are already in action. Some of us here will fumigate rat burrows and others will set up bait near storage bins. Others of our squads will be met by local health officials in the villages, and with the co-operation of the inhabitants we'll spray all living quarters, latrines, and refuse dumps.

By the control of pests we aim to save thousands of tons of food soon to be produced in the reclaimed areas. It wasn't so long ago, in fact as late as the sixties, that the world, hungry as it was, was losing three hundred million tons of food every year to worms and bugs. We've licked this thing in other places, and we're going to lick it here— Back to Control.

CONTROL: Got it. We're ready to make contact with the *Einstein,* which is carrying heads of various UN agencies and a party of official reporters. We transfer you now to Observer 8 aboard the *Einstein.* Over.

> *Interior of a custom-built jet. Its most striking feature is a plexiglass floor to the cabin, ribbed at intervals, but showing the ground in a very spectacular fashion.*

EINSTEIN: Got it, Control. We are flying low at about three thousand feet at low throttle. There's not much sound inside the cabin, although our ground speed must still be around four hundred miles per hour. This has been a swift and smooth flight from Pakistan.

We're just now arriving over the scene of the "invasion" here in the Tigris-Euphrates, and the whole lot of us are sitting forward and looking down through the plexiglass

106

floor, as you can see, like passengers in a glass-bottomed boat. At my right here is the chairman of the International Labor Organization—ILO—which has contributed so much to this day. I'm going to ask him to say a few words.

ILO CHAIRMAN: Well, all I can say is that the species of man has come a long way since the time when Nazis were making lampshades of human skin, and when the most urgent problem of science was to devise a bomb that could annihilate whole cities at a single stroke. What's going on down there thrills us in this ship because we've just flown over traces of the old roads and irrigation canals of thousands of years ago—a system smashed by invading Mongols in the thirteenth century. That's a lot different kind of invasion down there this morning, I'll tell you that! There's never been an army like this one. Nothing secret about it. Everybody knows its strength. These men don't have to worry about being bombed, or running into land mines; they're being greeted in villages and towns not by bullets and shells but by flowers and cheers. Some difference from the old style. Goodbye now.

EINSTEIN: We're losing speed and still more altitude in order to get a closer look at the activity, and we can plainly see construction crews starting to rebuild some of these ancient roads and canals. Here and there we can see ruins of old dams and levees along the river, but none of these will need to be restored, because of the new hydroelectric plant at Deir-ez-Zor, which we're going to inaugurate in a few minutes. (*With amusement*) Some of the tractors and truck units of the Task Force down there have recognized our plane and are flashing sun reflectors at us in greeting. We're tipping our wings in return greeting, and getting pretty much rocked about.

We've picked up speed now and are heading west toward the dam. On board with us here is a textile worker whose father, a bombardier with the Royal Air Force, was killed after destroying a dam on a mission over Nazi Germany. With poetic justice, there has fallen to this man the honor of *opening* the dam when we cross over it. I am going to ask him to say hello to you.

SON: Hello.

EINSTEIN: Is there anything you care to say to the people watching and listening around the world?

SON: (*Lancashire accent*) Well, I'm having a grand time. This is a jolly good show, and I'll certainly remember it for the rest of my life.

EINSTEIN: Thank you. Well, we are zooming toward the dam! There, as you can see, it stands clear and jewel-like in the sharp morning light. The lake formed by it is dazzling blue—and full of fish, they tell me. Been stocked with fish. Off to the south and east there you can see a network of canals and ditches that are going to fill up with life-giving water soon after the gates are opened. It's a matter of seconds now. The chief engineer of the dam is listening and he will pull the master switch as soon as he gets the verbal go-ahead. We are . . . just . . . now . . . crossing!

SON: Hello. Chief Engineer! Hit it! Open the gates!

> *The passengers, crowded to one side for a better view, almost block the camera's field, but a rift is made in time to see what the commentator describes:*

EINSTEIN: (*Excited*) There she blows! There's a beautiful stream of water, pouring through the penstock in a terrific torrent, the force of which you can sense even from up here! Now the generators in the power house are turning, and electricity will begin pulsing over the power lines to Damascus, Beirut, and as far away as Tel Aviv! I'm going to cut away momentarily to a ground camera—and mike

—down by the penstock, so that you can see and hear the water as it goes pouring through.

A flawless switchover. A Niagara of purposeful and determined water, making welcome thunder. Then, after a good look, back to the inside of the Einstein.

That's wealth pouring into this land! This harsh, dry earth, for centuries useless desert, will grow cotton, tobacco, wheat, sugar cane, corn, rice—and every bit of it will help make food abundant and cheap to millions of the world's hungry people who have hitherto lived under the constant shadow of famine. The Middle East, which for so many years was a depressed area of the world, will—

Cut off in mid-sentence. A rasping buzz, and a dead screen. Then Hill 1 comes in.

CONTROL: This is Control. We are very sorry about the interruption, but a bulldozer accidentally backed into one of our microwave relay units at Baiji and we lost the transmission from the *Einstein*. Nobody hurt, just a few broken tubes. Anyway, it's time to pick up the tower of an aero-generator in the hill country five hundred miles to the east—

Come in, Tower C-34. Over.

Perhaps the relay point at Baiji is missed, because the picture is a little fuzzy and unsteady. The signal must be coming roundabout. However, the audio portion is clear.

TOWER: This is Observer 9 standing in the generator room on top of Tower C-34, a sheer five hundred seventy-five feet above ground in a gap between hills. We're in an iso-

109

lated ridge here, and the wind really pushes when it gets going.

We've been listening to the broadcast from over the dam, and the very second those floodgates opened we started taking electricity right out of this forty-five-mile wind to feed into the power lines. This tower is only one of a series of ninety-two strung all the way up to Baku on the Caspian Sea and down to Kashan—a spread of over eight hundred miles.

The idea of these generators is to help out the hydro-electric systems up through this region, so that when the wind is blowing the dams won't have to work, and in that way they can accumulate water and avoid the danger of running low in the dry season.

That sound you hear in the background is the hum of a generator, drawing power from the turbine shafts— Well, I see a red light on my panel, which means to turn Control back to Hill 1.

Goodbye, everybody, from Aero-Generator Tower C-34. Over.

No trouble.

CONTROL: It is barely twenty minutes since dawn broke over this history-weary cradle of civilization, and already more new blood, energy, and wealth has come into this land than in the past twenty centuries.

You listeners and viewers throughout the world, who have paused in your celebration of this universal birthday to eavesdrop on the operation of Task Force One, must remember that the work of this morning merely inaugurates an enterprise that will continue for years, in ever-widening circles, until the whole world is benefited by peaceful construction. You have heard only the first twenty minutes out of the first eight hours of the first day

110

of the first Task Force. Westward across the world, in Brazil, Task Force Two awaits in darkness the rising of the sun seven hours from now. We now take you there.

This is Hill 1 on the Euphrates, saying "over" to Station 1 at Belém do Para, Brazil, South America. Over.

As an entirely different relay satellite is involved, there is a delay of a few seconds before workable contact is made with Belém. Then, we see a commentator speaking from a grassy area near the bank of the Amazon, the scene lit by kleig lights in which hundreds of insects are going quite mad.

BELEM: It is night here at Belém, and Task Force Two, a force so big it is split up into three sections a thousand miles apart from each other, is sleeping.

Here at the mouth of the Amazon, the first section will be up and in action by dawn. The force at Station 2 in Manaos, a thousand miles inland, will follow when the sun reaches there an hour later; and Section 3, at Iquitos, Peru, another fifteen hundred miles further upstream, will enter the Blitz on the third hour.

Before the end of the day in South America, the massive Yangtze Blitz in China will be on, in the hands of World Task Force Three; and world-wide broadcasts similar to the one you have just heard from the Tigris-Euphrates will bring you a description of the successive invasions—

And now, ladies and gentlemen, the Co-ordinator of World Task Force Two:

A woman in her late thirties, rather pretty in a Latin way. Not, as you might expect, a Lachaise female with mighty biceps and a

111

Gibraltar bottom. The minute she speaks,
you know she was not made co-ordinator be-
cause she knew somebody high up.

CO-ORDINATOR 2: I wish only to express the supreme confidence of this Force, that the difficulties facing us in the vast Amazon basin—an area almost as large as that of the United States or Australia—will be overcome.

The obstacles which have frustrated all previous national expeditions in Amazonia are certainly not trivial, but neither are they insurmountable. With the help of the peoples of all nations, working together through the UN, we will render these three million square miles into one of the world's greatest food reserves, we will eliminate tropical diseases, clear jungles, build airfields, dig mines, stock the ranges, harness the unimaginable power of the Amazon and its tributaries, establish industries and cities, and pour the latent riches of this continent into the bloodstream of world prosperity.

We salute our brothers and sisters in Task Forces One and Three, and send a greeting to every stockholder in this enterprise—which means to each last individual on the face of the earth.

BELEM: We return you to United Nations Headquarters. Over.

Cheering. Heavy cheering. The view from
the rooftop. Observer 1 has to raise his voice
to be heard, since even those around him on
the platform are applauding, and it continues.

OBSERVER 1: This is Observer 1 on the roof of UN Headquarters in New York. A cheering, shouting throng is voicing its appreciation of the dramatic efficiency with which the first gunless, bloodless, and creative Blitz in the history of the world is taking place without impediment

112

in the oldest civilized region on earth. The grounds of the UN Headquarters are surging with people. They are clamoring for the appearance of the General Secretary, the President of the Assembly, and international delegations . . . I believe their wish is to be granted, because I can see some of the delegates beginning to leave their places and—

> *His voice, and the tumultuous cheering, have been steadily fading over the last fifteen seconds of the foregoing, and now they can be heard no more.*
>
> *There is a weighty, unhappy silence. Then, the same voice we heard at the beginning:*

VOICE: A dream, a dream, a dream!

We awaken rudely, we leave the future behind, we return to the present, and nobody is cheering. The longing of the peoples for peace and amity waits outside the armored door of events like a man applying for relief, hat in hand.

The Peace Blitz and the World Task Force are off in the milky distances of the stars, and here on earth squat hunger and poverty, disease, erosion, and the armed camps. In the Middle East, the Tiger and Euphrates coil sluggishly tonight; no new villages rise, no turbines spin; the marshes breed malaria and the people are sick. In the deep of Brazil the Amazon slumbers, and the wealth of the continent stays hidden.

Between what could be and what is are barbed wire and tank traps, walls, armed borders, reconnaissance patrols, old wounds and new suspicions, hatred, fear, corruption, ignorance, intolerance, cold war, threats of hot war, fallout, trouble compounded into trouble, for details of which consult your morning newspaper.

But there is also a hope, and more than a hope, and what could be may one day break through and become. At least one part of the dream is true—all those dams, wind towers, seeding planes, heat pumps, atomic piles, the radar on the fishing boats, the techniques, the manpower, the international agencies, the funds—they're all here *now;* and in some instances co-operation has already begun among nations, through the UN itself.

Could it be, then? Could this fantasy in which peace and co-operation are more exciting to the world than war—could this possibly be?

If a man foreseeing the airplane and telephone and atom bomb a hundred years ago had told an audience of sensible, practical citizens:

PROPHET: Man, born of earth and water and a touch of fire, custom-sodden before his whiskers show, trading sweat and curses and marketable goods, leaping to war at the whisper of a drum, dreaming dreams, yet stoning the prophets who pronounce them!

This man will one day fly sturdier than the eagle, higher and farther and faster. He will swim at the side of the whale, under whole seas. He will throw his voice instantly across mountains, rivers, and plains, yet speak quietly and to a single ear. He will take two buckets of cold metal, dancing with atoms, and spark them, and cities will crash to earth!

VOICE: They would have laughed him out of town, or fetched him to the asylum. Will they laugh now when he says:

PROPHET: Man will gather the nations under one roof; and by their acts and counsels, warring shall cease in far places, and the hardships of peoples shall be eased, and the earth shall prosper, and there shall be good will.

VOICE: (*Quietly*) Is it possible? Could it be?

ABOUT THE AUTHOR

NORMAN CORWIN, who has long been concerned with the problems of our nuclear age, has led a distinguished career in almost every area of the communicative arts. Born in Boston, he went straight from high school into newspaper work, became a radio and film critic, joined CBS in 1938 to write, direct, and produce some of the memorable broadcasts in the history of radio. Three collections of his plays were published under the titles *Thirteen by Corwin, More by Corwin,* and *Untitled.* For three years he served as Chief of Special Projects for United Nations Radio; subsequently he has written films for RKO, MGM, and 20th Century-Fox; a novella, *Dog in the Sky;* and two plays (*The Rivalry,* 1959, and *The World of Carl Sandburg,* 1961) which he also directed; both toured the country and played on Broadway. Mr. Corwin is married, has two children, and lives in California.

This book was set in
Times Roman and Univers types by
Harry Sweetman Typesetting Corporation.
It was printed and bound at the press of
The World Publishing Company.
Design is by Jack Jaget.

70
71
72
74
75
76
77
79
83
85
89